# About the Author

Paul Watson is a technology enthusiast and has massive experience in various technologies like web application development, automation testing, build automation, continuous integration and deployment technologies. He has worked on most of the technology stacks.
He has hands on experience on UFT, LeanFT, Selenium and Appium. He has used testing frameworks like JUnit, TestNG, Cucumber with Selenium. He has also worked on Struts, Spring, Bootstratp, Angular JS.

His hobbies include travelling to new tourist places, watching basketball, cricket and learning latest technological stuff.

## A special note of thanks to my Wife

I would like to dedicate this book to my lovely wife for loving me so much and helping me write this book. Without her support, this book would not have been a reality.

# Who this book is for

This book is for automation engineers who want to learn Selenium in PHP to automate the web applications.

It is assumed that reader has basic programming skills in PHP language. Whether you are a beginner or an experienced developer, this book will help you master the skills on Selenium in PHP.

The book starts with introduction of Selenium and then dives into key concepts as mentioned below.

1. Launching browsers with Desired Capabilities – Chrome, Chrome with options, Chrome in Mobile Emulation, IE, Firefox
2. Element Identification – Element identification methods, Advanced XPATH expressions, Advanced CSS selectors
3. Assertions in Selenium in PHP
4. Interacting with elements in Selenium in PHP
5. Basic Browser window automation
6. Sending keys in Selenium in PHP
7. Synchronization in Selenium
8. Check if Element exists
9. Working with Tables using Selenium
10. Performing advanced actions using Selenium in PHP
11. Executing JavaScript in Selenium in PHP
12. Switching contexts – Working with multiple Browser Windows or tabs, Working with multiple frames, Handling alerts

13. Common exceptions in Selenium
14. Frameworks in Selenium – Taking a screenshot in selenium, Mocha – Unit testing framework
15. Selenium grid

# Table of Contents

# 1. Introduction to Selenium Webdriver

Selenium Webdriver is the industry leading web automation testing tool.

Main features of Selenium are given below.

1. Open source
2. Cross platform
3. Automates all major browsers like Internet Explorer, Microsoft edge, Google chrome, Firefox, Safari, Opera
4. We can write the tests in various languages like Java, Groovy, C#.Net, VB.Net, PHP, PHP, Python, Ruby, Perl, objective C and many more!
5. Runs on JSON webdriver protocol over HTTP

Below image shows how the Selenium Webdriver protocol works.

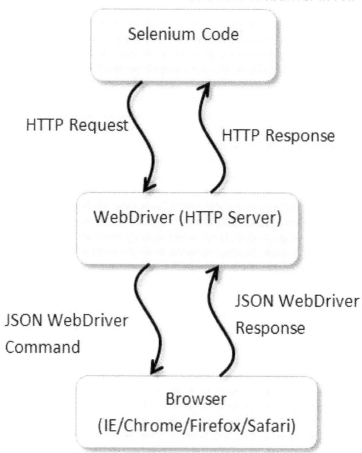

Selenium Webdriver Protocol

# 2. Installation and Environment set up

We would be using selenium client API developed by Facebook.

The API documentation is available at http://facebook.github.io/php-webdriver/

The API is similar to the one in Java. We would be using PHPUnit as a testing framework to write the Selenium tests.

1.  Install PHP with WAMP.
2.  Download and start Selenium server
3.  Install Selenium client package provided by Facebook

## Installation of WAMP

After installation of WAMP, you need to update the PATH variable to include the PHP directory .( e.g. "C:\wamp64\bin\php\php7.0.10")

Below command can be used to see which ini file is being used by PHP.

```
php --ini
```

Below command can be used to view the php info

```
php -n -c /conf -r'phpinfo();'
```

Below command is used to view which modules have been loaded by php

```
php -m
```

You can find out where the PHP is installed using below command in windows.

```
where php.exe
```

## Download and start Selenium server

We also need the Selenium standalone server to be running before we start automating browsers. You can download and start the server using below command.

```
java -jar selenium-standalone-server.jar
```

Install Selenium client package provided by Facebook

Create composer.json file with below contents in your working directory.

```
{
"require-dev": {
"phpunit/phpunit": "*",
"facebook/webdriver": "dev-master"
}
}
```

https://packagist.org/ is the package manager for PHP just like how we have a NPM for PHP

Then download composer.phar file from below location.

```
https://getcomposer.org/composer.phar
```

Then execute below command to install all required libraries.

```
php composer.phar install
```

Before you execute above command, you will have to enable PHP's openssl extension. Otherwise, you will get below error.

```
The openssl extension is required for
SSL/TLS protection but is not available.
```

All library files are downloaded and stored in vendor directory as shown in below image.

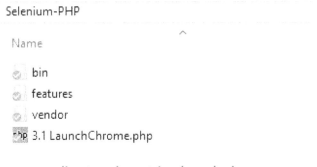

Selenium-PHP

Name

bin
features
vendor
3.1 LaunchChrome.php

directory-layout-in-php-selenium

## 3. Launching browsers with Desired Capabilities

### 3.1 Launching Chrome browser

Below example illustrates how to launch the chrome browser using Selenium in PHP. You may get error saying "WebDriverCurlException - Curl error thrown for http POST to /session with params". To avoid this error, make sure that you have installed latest driver exe files.

```php
<?php
class LaunchChrome extends
PHPUnit_Framework_TestCase

{

protected $driver;

public function setUp()
{
$capabilities =
array(\WebDriverCapabilityType::BROWSER_NAM
E => 'chrome');
$this->driver =
RemoteWebDriver::create('http://localhost:4
444/wd/hub', $capabilities);
}

public function testLaunchChrome()
{
$this->driver-
>get("http://www.softpost.org");
// checking that page title contains word
'Tutorial'
```

```php
$this->assertContains('Tutorial', $this-
>driver->getTitle());
}

public function tearDown()
{
//Quit the driver
$this->driver->quit();
}
}

//To execute this test, you need to use
below command.
//vendor/bin/phpunit LaunchChrome.php
?>
```

## 3.2 Launching chrome with options

Below example shows how to launch the chrome browser
with various options (arguments) in Selenium in PHP.

```php
<?php
class LaunchChrome extends
PHPUnit_Framework_TestCase

{

protected $driver;

public function setUp()
{
$options = new ChromeOptions();

// Use different chrome binary
```

```php
//$options->setBinary('/path_to_binary');

//Setting Arguments for the chrome browser


$options->addArguments(array(
'--disable-extensions',
'start-maximized',
'disable-popup-blocking',
'test-type'
));

//Add extensions for chrome browser


$options->addExtensions(array(
//give path to .crx extension file',
));

$caps = DesiredCapabilities::chrome();
$caps-
>setCapability(ChromeOptions::CAPABILITY,
$options);
$this->driver =
RemoteWebDriver::create('http://localhost:4
444/wd/hub', $caps);
}

public function testChromeOptions()
{
$this->driver-
>get("http://www.softpost.org");
```

```
// checking that page title contains word
'Tutorial'

$this->assertContains('Tutorial', $this-
>driver->getTitle());
}

public function tearDown()
{


//Quit the driver


$this->driver->quit();
}
}
?>
```

## 3.3 Chrome in Mobile Emulation

Below example shows how to start the chrome with Mobile Emulation mode using Selenium in PHP.

```php
<?php
class MyTest extends
PHPUnit_Framework_TestCase
{
protected $driver;

public function setUp()
{
$options = new ChromeOptions();

// Use different chrome binary

//$options->setBinary('/path_to_binary');

//Setting Arguments for the chrome browser

$options->addArguments(array(
'--disable-extensions',
'start-maximized',
'disable-popup-blocking',
'test-type'
));
$mobile_emulation = [ "deviceName" =>
"Apple iPhone 6" ];

//$mobile_emulation = [ "deviceName" =>
"Apple iPhone 5" ];

//$mobile_emulation = [ "deviceName" =>
"Google Nexus 5" ];
```

```php
$options-
>setExperimentalOption("mobileEmulation",
$mobile_emulation);
$caps = DesiredCapabilities::chrome();
$caps-
>setCapability(ChromeOptions::CAPABILITY,
$options);
$this->driver =
RemoteWebDriver::create('http://localhost:4
444/wd/hub', $caps);
}
public function testEmulation()
{
$this->driver-
>get("http://www.softpost.org/selenium-
test-page");

$mainHandle = $this->driver-
>getWindowHandle();
echo ("\n Main window handle -> " .
$mainHandle );
}
public function tearDown()
{

//Quit the driver

$this->driver->quit();
}
}
?>
```

## 3.4 Launching IE

Below example illustrates how to launch Internet Explorer in Selenium in PHP. Make sure that protected mode settings are same for all zones in IE before running the code. Also IEDriverserver.exe file should be in PATH.

```php
<?php
class LaunchIE extends
PHPUnit_Framework_TestCase

{

protected $webDriver;

public function setUp()
{
$capabilities =
array(\WebDriverCapabilityType::BROWSER_NAM
E => 'internet explorer');
$this->webDriver =
RemoteWebDriver::create('http://localhost:4
444/wd/hub', $capabilities);
}

protected $url = 'http://www.softpost.org';

public function testTitle()
{
$this->webDriver->get($this->url);

// checking that page title contains word
'Tutorial'
```

```php
$this->assertContains('Tutorial', $this-
>webDriver->getTitle());
}
public function tearDown()
{

//Close the browser

$this->webDriver->quit();
}
}
?>
```

## 3.5 Launch Firefox

Below example illustrates how to launch the Firefox
browser using Selenium in PHP. Note that you will have to
add the Geckodriver in system PATH to be able to
automate latest Firefox with Selenium 3.0 and above.

```php
<?php
class LaunchFirefox extends
PHPUnit_Framework_TestCase
{
protected $webDriver;

public function setUp()
{
$capabilities =
array(\WebDriverCapabilityType::BROWSER_NAM
E => 'firefox');
$this->webDriver =
RemoteWebDriver::create('http://localhost:4
444/wd/hub', $capabilities);
}
```

```php
protected $url = 'http://www.softpost.org';

public function testTitle()
{
$this->webDriver->get($this->url);

// checking that page title contains word
'Tutorial'
$this->assertContains('Tutorial', $this-
>webDriver->getTitle());
}

public function tearDown()
{
//Close the browser
$this->webDriver->quit();
}
}
?>
```

# 4. Element Identification

## 4.1 Element identification methods

We can identify the web elements using below Element locators in PHP

1. className
2. tagName
3. name
4. id
5. xpath
6. css
7. linkText
8. partialLinkText

```
WebDriverBy::className()
WebDriverBy::tagName()
WebDriverBy::name()
WebDriverBy::id()
WebDriverBy::xpath()
WebDriverBy::cssSelector()
WebDriverBy::linkText()
WebDriverBy::partialLinkText()
```

findElements method returns an array of elements. This method returns all elements matching given locator.

Below example demonstrates how to use findElements method in Selenium in PHP.

```php
<?php

class LinkTest extends
PHPUnit_Framework_TestCase

{

protected $webDriver;

public function setUp()
{
$capabilities =
array(\WebDriverCapabilityType::BROWSER_NAM
E => 'chrome');
$this->webDriver =
RemoteWebDriver::create('http://localhost:4
444/wd/hub', $capabilities);
}

public function tearDown()
{

$this->webDriver->quit();
}

public function testLink()
{
$this->webDriver-
>get("http://www.softpost.org");
```

```php
//Show all links containing selenium on
page
$links = $this->webDriver-
>findElements(WebDriverBy::partialLinkText(
'Selenium'));
foreach($links as $link)
{
echo ("\n" . $link->getAttribute('href') .
"\n");
}

//find and click Selenium link
$seleniumLink = $this->webDriver-
>findElement(WebDriverBy::linkText('Seleniu
m'));
$seleniumLink->click();

$this->webDriver->close();
}
}

?>
```

## 4.2 Advanced XPATH expressions

## What is xpath in selenium web driver?

xpath is used to find the specific element in the given
webpage.

Some of the below examples will demonstrate how we can
write the xpath expressions.

| Find all elements with tag input | //input |
|---|---|
| Find all input tag element having attribute type = 'hidden' | //input[@type='hidden'] |
| Find all input tag element having attribute type = 'hidden' and name attribute = 'ren' | //input[@type='hidden'][@name='ren'] |
| Find all input tag element with attribute type containing 'hid' | //input[contains(@type,'hid')] |
| Find all input tag element with attribute type starting with 'hid' | //input[starts-with(@type,'hid')] |
| Find all elements | //*[text()='Password'] |

| | |
|---|---|
| having innertext = 'password' | |
| Find all td elements having innertext = 'password' | //td[text()='Password'] |
| Find all next siblings of td tag having innertext = 'gender' | //td[text()='Gender']//following-sibling::* |
| Find all elements in the 2nd next sibling of td tag having innertext = 'gender' | //td[text()='Gender']//following-sibling::*[2]//* |
| Find input elements in the 2nd next sibling of td tag having innertext = 'gender' | //td[text()='Gender']//following-sibling::*[2]//input |

| | |
|---|---|
| Find the td which contains font element containing the text '12' | //td[font[contains(text(),'12')]] |
| Find all the preceding siblings of the td which contains font element containing the text '12' | //td[font[contains(text(),'12')]]//preceding-sibling::* |
| Find the second td ancestor of the span element containing text - Exp Date then find the previous td element' | //span[text()='Exp Date']//ancestor::td[2]//preceding-sibling::td |
| Find the first td ancestor of the span element containing text - Exp Date then find the previous td | //span[text()='Exp Date']//ancestor::td[1]//preceding-sibling::td |

| | |
|---|---|
| element | |
| Find the element containing specific text | //p[text()[contains(.,'refer')]] |

Below example shows how to use logical operators (and / or / not) in XPATH.

```
//div[contains(@class,'result-row') and not
(contains(@style,'none'))]
```

Below example shows how to handle the quote inside text

```
//label[contains(text(),"Killer\'s age.")]
```

## 4.3 Advanced CSS selectors

### What is CssSelector in selenium web driver?

cssSelector is used to find the specific element in the given webpage.

Some of the below examples will demonstrate how we can write the cssSelector expressions.

| | |
|---|---|
| Find all elements with tag input | input |
| Find all input tag element having attribute type = 'hidden' | input[type='hidden'] |
| Find all input tag element having attribute type = 'hidden' and name attribute = 'ren' | input[type='hidden'][name='ren'] |
| Find all input tag element with attribute type containing 'hid' | input[type*='hid'] |
| Find all input tag element with attribute type starting with 'hid' | input[type^='hid'] |
| Find all input tag element with attribute type ending with 'den' | input[type$='den'] |

You can find the element containing specific text using below CSS Selector syntax.

```
$("h3:contains('Cloud')")
```

Above css will select the element H3 containing text Cloud

## 5. Assertions in Selenium in PHP

We can use Assertion library provided in PHPUnit as shown in below example.

```php
<?php

class AssertionTest extends
PHPUnit_Framework_TestCase
{
protected $webDriver;

public function setUp()
{
$capabilities =
array(\WebDriverCapabilityType::BROWSER_NAM
E => 'chrome');
$this->webDriver =
RemoteWebDriver::create('http://localhost:4
444/wd/hub', $capabilities);
}

public function tearDown()
{

$this->webDriver->quit();
}

public function testLink()
{
$this->webDriver-
>get("http://www.softpost.org/selenium-
test-page");
$this->assertContains('Tutorial', $this-
>webDriver->getTitle());
$this->assertTrue('Selenium Test Page |
```

```
Free Software Tutorials'==$this->webDriver-
>getTitle());
$this->assertFalse('Selenium Test Page |
Free Software Tutorials'!=$this->webDriver-
>getTitle());
$this->assertEquals('Selenium Test Page |
Free Software Tutorials', $this->webDriver-
>getTitle());
$this->assertSame('Selenium Test Page |
Free Software Tutorials', $this->webDriver-
>getTitle());
$this->assertGreaterThan(2,4,"Verifying
that 4 is greater than 2");
$this->assertGreaterThanOrEqual(2,4,"");
$this->assertLessThan(14,12,"");
$this->assertLessThanOrEqual(14,12,"");
$this->webDriver->close();
}
}

?>
```

# 6. Interacting with elements in Selenium in PHP

Below example demonstrates how to interact with web elements using Selenium in PHP.

1. Sending keys
2. Clearing the text box
3. Getting value from text box
4. Selecting value from drop down
5. Checking if element is disabled/enabled
6. Checking if element is selected or not selected

```php
<?php
class MyTest extends
PHPUnit_Framework_TestCase
{
protected $driver;
public function setUp()
{
$capabilities =
array(\WebDriverCapabilityType::BROWSER_NAM
E => 'chrome');
$this->driver =
RemoteWebDriver::create('http://localhost:4
444/wd/hub', $capabilities);
$this->driver->manage()->window()-
>maximize();
}
public function testInteractions()
{
$this->driver-
>get("http://www.softpost.org/selenium-
test-page");
```

```php
$this->driver-
>findElement(WebDriverBy::id('fn'))-
>sendKeys('Shaun');
//$this->driver-
>findElement(WebDriverBy::id('fn'))-
>click();
//$this->driver->getKeyboard()-
>sendKeys('Shaun');
$firstName = $this->driver-
>findElement(WebDriverBy::id('fn'))-
>getAttribute('value');
$this->assertEquals('Shaun', $firstName);
$this->driver-
>findElement(WebDriverBy::id('fn'))-
>clear();
$this->driver-
>findElement(WebDriverBy::id('fn'))-
>sendKeys('Hyden');
$this->driver-
>findElement(WebDriverBy::xpath("//input[@v
alue='QTP']"))->click();
sleep(1);

//To get value of an attribute of an element,
use getAttribute(attributeName) method.

$attribute = $this->driver-
>findElement(WebDriverBy::linkText('Seleniu
m in Java'))->getAttribute('href');
echo("\n href attribute of Link is " .
$attribute);

//To check if an element is enabled, use
isEnabled() method.

$enabled = $this->driver-
>findElement(WebDriverBy::xpath("//input[@v
```

```
alue='QTP']"))->isEnabled();
echo("\n QTP checkbox is enabled? " .
$enabled);

//To check if an element is enabled, use
isSelected() method.

$selected = $this->driver-
>findElement(WebDriverBy::xpath("//input[@v
alue='QTP']"))->isSelected();
echo("\n QTP checkbox is selected? " .
$selected);

//To get the text of an element, use getText()
method.

$txt = $this->driver-
>findElement(WebDriverBy::tagName("p"))-
>getText();
echo("\n Text in first paragraph -> " .
$txt);

//To get the text of an element, use getText()
method.

$displayed = $this->driver-
>findElement(WebDriverBy::xpath("//input[@v
alue='Sign up']"))->isDisplayed();
echo("\n is Sign up button displayed? -> "
. $displayed);

//To get css value of an element , use
getCssValue() method.
//To get tag name of an element , use
getTagName() method.

$tagName = $this->driver-
>findElement(WebDriverBy::linkText('Seleniu
```

33

```php
m in Java'))->getTagName();
echo("\nTagName of Link is " . $tagName);

//Select city from the dropdown

$this->driver-
>findElement(WebDriverBy::xpath("//select//
option[text()='Mumbai']"))->click();
sleep(2);

//We can also use WebDriverSelect class to work
with drop downs

$dropDown = $this->driver-
>findElement(WebDriverBy::xpath("//select")
);
(new WebDriverSelect($dropDown))-
>selectByVisibleText("Pune");

//You can use below methods of WebDriverSelect
class

//isMultiple(), getOptions(),
getAllSelectedOptions(),
getFirstSelectedOption()
//deselectAll(), selectByIndex(),
selectByValue(), selectByVisibleText()
//deselectByIndex(), deselectByValue(),
deselectByVisibleText(), escapeQuotes()
echo ("\nThe selected option is -> " . (new
WebDriverSelect($dropDown))-
>getFirstSelectedOption()->getText());
sleep(2);
}
public function tearDown()
{

//Quit the driver
```

```
$this->driver->quit();
}
}
?>
```

# 7. Basic Browser window automation, Sending keys in Selenium in PHP

Below example shows how to perform basic Browser window automation. We are performing below things.

1. Navigating backward and forward
2. Resizing the window
3. Getting page source
4. Getting current page title and url

```php
<?php
class MyTest extends
PHPUnit_Framework_TestCase
{
protected $webDriver;
public function setUp()
{
$capabilities =
array(\WebDriverCapabilityType::BROWSER_NAM
E => 'chrome');
$this->webDriver =
RemoteWebDriver::create('http://localhost:4
444/wd/hub', $capabilities);
$this->webDriver->manage()->window()-
>maximize();
}
public function testBrowser()
{
$this->webDriver-
>get("http://www.softpost.org/selenium-
test-page");

//We can use below code to navigate forward and
backward.
```

```php
$this->webDriver->navigate()->back();
$this->webDriver->navigate()->forward();
$this->webDriver->manage()->window()-
>setSize(new WebDriverDimension(300,300));
echo ("\nCurrent Page Source -> " . $this-
>webDriver->getPageSource());
echo ("\nCurrent title -> " . $this-
>webDriver->getTitle());
echo ("\nCurrent URL -> " . $this-
>webDriver->getCurrentUrl());
}
public function tearDown()
{

//Quit the driver

$this->webDriver->quit();
}
}
?>
```

## Sending keys in Selenium

Below example shows how to press various keys in Selenium in PHP.

```php
<?php
class MyTest extends
PHPUnit_Framework_TestCase
{
protected $webDriver;
public function setUp()
{
$capabilities =
array(\WebDriverCapabilityType::BROWSER_NAM
E => 'chrome');
$this->webDriver =
RemoteWebDriver::create('http://localhost:4
444/wd/hub', $capabilities);
$this->webDriver->manage()->window()-
>maximize();
}
public function testKeys()
{
$this->webDriver-
>get("http://www.softpost.org/selenium-
test-page");
$this->webDriver-
>findElement(WebDriverBy::id('fn'))-
>sendKeys("Ponting");
sleep(2);

//Sending combination of characters

$this->webDriver-
>findElement(WebDriverBy::id('fn'))-
>sendKeys(WebDriverKeys::CONTROL . "a");
sleep(2);
```

```php
//Similarly you can press any other key as
mentioned below

//CANCEL, BACKSPACE, TAB, RETURN_KEY,
ENTER, SHIFT, ALT, ESCAPE, SPACE
//PAGE_UP, PAGE_DOWN, END, HOME,
ARROW_LEFT, UP, DOWN, ARROW_UP, INSERT,
DELETE, NUMPAD0
//F1 to F12
}
public function tearDown()
{

//Quit the driver

$this->webDriver->quit();
}
}
?>
```

# 8. Synchronization in Selenium, Check if Element exists

## Synchronization

Below example shows how to add synchronization in Selenium in PHP.

```php
<?php
class MyTest extends
PHPUnit_Framework_TestCase
{
protected $driver;
public function setUp()
{
$capabilities =
array(\WebDriverCapabilityType::BROWSER_NAM
E => 'chrome');
$this->driver =
RemoteWebDriver::create('http://localhost:4
444/wd/hub', $capabilities);
$this->driver->manage()->window()-
>maximize();
}
public function testSynchronization()
{
$this->driver->manage()->timeouts()-
>implicitlyWait(20);
$this->driver->manage()->timeouts()-
>setScriptTimeout(10);
$this->driver->manage()->timeouts()-
>pageLoadTimeout(60);
$this->driver-
>get("http://www.softpost.org/selenium-
test-page");
```

```
//Now let us see what is explicit timeouts
//We can provide specific condition in explicit
wait
//Below code will wait for maximum 20 seconds
checking the title of page.
//If title does not become the expected one
after 20 seconds, Timeout exception is thrown
```

```php
$this->driver->wait(20, 100)-
>until(WebDriverExpectedCondition::titleIs(
'Selenium Test Page | Free Software
Tutorials'));
```

```
//Below statement will force the driver to wait
until link is visible.
```

```php
$this->driver->wait(20, 100)-
>until(WebDriverExpectedCondition::visibili
tyOfElementLocated(WebDriverBy::linkText('S
elenium in Java')));
```

```
//You can use many conditions as mentioned
below.
```

```php
//titleContains(),
presenceOfElementLocated(),
visibilityOfElementLocated()
//visibilityOf(),
presenceOfAllElementsLocatedBy(),
textToBePresentInElement()
//textToBePresentInElementValue(),
frameToBeAvailableAndSwitchToIt(),
invisibilityOfElementLocated()
//invisibilityOfElementWithText(),
elementToBeClickable(), stalenessOf(),
refreshed()
//elementToBeSelected(),
elementSelectionStateToBe(),
```

```
alertIsPresent()
}
public function tearDown()
{

//Quit the driver

$this->driver->quit();
}
}
?>
```

## Check if Element exists

Below example shows how to check if specific element exists on the web page or not.

```
<?php
class TestSize extends
PHPUnit_Framework_TestCase
{
protected $webDriver;
public function setUp()
{
$capabilities =
array(\WebDriverCapabilityType::BROWSER_NAM
E => 'chrome');
$this->webDriver =
RemoteWebDriver::create('http://localhost:4
444/wd/hub', $capabilities);
$this->webDriver->manage()->window()-
>maximize();
}
public function testSize()
{
```

```php
$this->webDriver-
>get("http://www.softpost.org/selenium-
test-page");
$elements = $this->webDriver-
>findElements(WebDriverBy::id('fn'));
if (sizeof($elements)==0)
echo("\n Element with id fn not found");
else
echo("\n Element with id fn found");
}
public function tearDown()
{

//Quit the driver

$this->webDriver->quit();
}
}
?>
```

# 9. Working with Tables using Selenium

In this topic, You will learn how to perform below operations on table using Selenium.

1. Find total number of rows and columns in a table
2. Read a value from the table cell
3. Click on elements inside table cells

## Finding total number of rows and columns in a table

1. //table//tr – This XPATH can be used to get all tr elements inside the table. Note that if there are nested tables, it will get all nested tr elements as well. To get only immediate child tr elements, you will have to use children property which returns collection of child tr elements. Alternatively you can use "//table/tr" XPATH to find only immediate child tr elements. Note that we have used single / which means find only immediate children.

2. //table//th -This XPATH can be used to find total number of columns in a table. Note that all column headings should be marked with th tag. Also note that if one th tag spans multiple columns, it will be counted only once.

3. //table//tr[1]//td – This XPATH finds all td elements (table cells) in the first row of the table. Note that all nested td elements will be found using this XPATH expression.

## 10. Performing advanced actions using Selenium in PHP

Below example shows how to perform complex actions using Selenium in PHP like drag and drop, moving to element, double clicking on an element, right clicking on an element etc.

```php
<?php
class MyTest extends
PHPUnit_Framework_TestCase
{
protected $webDriver;
public function setUp()
{
$capabilities =
array(\WebDriverCapabilityType::BROWSER_NAM
E => 'chrome');
$this->webDriver =
RemoteWebDriver::create('http://localhost:4
444/wd/hub', $capabilities);
$this->webDriver->manage()->window()-
>maximize();
}
public function testActions()
{
$this->webDriver-
>get("http://www.softpost.org/selenium-
test-page");
$e1 = $this->webDriver-
>findElement(WebDriverBy::id('fn'));
$e2 = $this->webDriver-
>findElement(WebDriverBy::linkText('Seleniu
m in Java'));
$action = new WebDriverActions($this-
>webDriver);
$action->moveToElement($e1)->click($e2)-
```

```
>perform();
sleep(3);

//Similarly you can perform below actions.

//clickAndHold(), contextClick(),
doubleClick()
//dragAndDrop(), dragAndDropBy(),
moveByOffset(), moveToElement()
//keyDown(), keyUp(), release(), sendKeys()
}
public function tearDown()
{

//Quit the driver

$this->webDriver->quit();
}
}
?>
```

# 11. Executing JavaScript in Selenium in PHP

Below example shows how to execute the JavaScript in Selenium in PHP.

```php
<?php
class MyTest extends
PHPUnit_Framework_TestCase
{
protected $driver;
public function setUp()
{
$capabilities =
array(\WebDriverCapabilityType::BROWSER_NAM
E => 'chrome');
$this->driver =
RemoteWebDriver::create('http://localhost:4
444/wd/hub', $capabilities);
$this->driver->manage()->window()-
>maximize();
}
public function testJS()
{
$this->driver-
>get("http://www.softpost.org/selenium-
test-page");
$src = $this->driver->executeScript('return
document.body.innerHTML;');
echo ("Source of page -> " . $src);

//click on the radio button using java script
//Notice how we have passed the argument to the
java script code.

$elements = $this->driver-
>findElements(WebDriverBy::xpath("//input[@
value='female']"));
$this->driver-
```

```php
>executeScript('arguments[0].click();',$ele
ments);
sleep(2);
}
public function tearDown()
{

//Quit the driver

$this->driver->quit();
}
}
?>
```

# 12. Switching contexts

## 12.1 Working with multiple Browser Windows or tabs

Below example shows how to Work with multiple Browser Windows or tabs in Selenium in PHP.

```php
<?php
class MyTest extends
PHPUnit_Framework_TestCase
{
protected $driver;
public function setUp()
{
$capabilities =
array(\WebDriverCapabilityType::BROWSER_NAM
E => 'chrome');
$this->driver =
RemoteWebDriver::create('http://localhost:4
444/wd/hub', $capabilities);
$this->driver->manage()->window()-
>maximize();
}
public function testBrowserWindows()
{
$this->driver-
>get("http://www.softpost.org/selenium-
test-page");
$mainHandle = $this->driver-
>getWindowHandle();
echo ("\n Main window handle -> " .
$mainHandle );
$this->driver-
>findElement(WebDriverBy::linkText("Seleniu
m in Java"))->click();
```

```php
$HandleSet = $this->driver-
>getWindowHandles();
echo ("\n Total count of window handles ->
" . sizeof($HandleSet) );

//Switching to the popup window.

foreach( $HandleSet as $handle)
{
if($handle!=$mainHandle)
{

//Switch to newly created window

echo ("\n window handle of new window -> "
. $handle );
$this->driver->switchTo()->window($handle);
echo ("\n Title of new window -> " . $this-
>driver->getTitle() );
}
}
}
public function tearDown()
{

//Quit the driver

$this->driver->quit();
}
}
?>
```

## 12.2 Working with multiple frames

Below example explains how to switch to frame in
Selenium in PHP. In below example, we are switching to
frame with name "g" and grabbing the portion of page
source inside that frame. Then we have switched to main
window document using defaultContent() method.

```php
<?php
class MyTest extends
PHPUnit_Framework_TestCase
{
protected $webDriver;
public function setUp()
{
$capabilities =
array(\WebDriverCapabilityType::BROWSER_NAM
E => 'chrome');
$this->webDriver =
RemoteWebDriver::create('http://localhost:4
444/wd/hub', $capabilities);
$this->webDriver->manage()->window()-
>maximize();
}
public function testFrames()
{
$this->webDriver-
>get("http://www.softpost.org/selenium-
test-page");
//Switch to frame with name "g"
$this->webDriver->switchTo()->frame("g");
echo ("\nPortion of HTML Source of Frame ->
" . substr($this->webDriver-
>getPageSource(), 0, 300));
echo
("\n\n*********************************
*****************************\n");
```

```php
$this->webDriver->switchTo()-
>defaultContent();
echo ("\nPortion of HTML Source of Main
window -> " . substr($this->webDriver-
>getPageSource(), 0, 300));
}
public function tearDown()
{

//Quit the driver

$this->webDriver->quit();
}
}
?>
```

## 12.3 Handling alerts

Below example shows how to handle alerts in Selenium in
PHP.

```php
<?php
class MyTest extends
PHPUnit_Framework_TestCase
{
protected $driver;
public function setUp()
{
$capabilities =
array(\WebDriverCapabilityType::BROWSER_NAM
E => 'chrome');
$this->driver =
RemoteWebDriver::create('http://localhost:4
444/wd/hub', $capabilities);
$this->driver->manage()->window()-
>maximize();
}
```

```php
public function testAlerts()
{
$this->driver-
>get("http://www.softpost.org/selenium-
test-page");
try
{

//To accept alert, you can use below line
of code

$this->driver->switchTo()->alert()-
>accept();

//To dismiss alert, you can use below line
of code

$this->driver->switchTo()->alert()-
>dismiss();
}
catch(Exception $ex)
{
echo ("Exception occured while trying to
accept the alert" . $ex->getMessage());
}
}
public function tearDown()
{

//Quit the driver

$this->driver->quit();
}
}
?>
```

# 13. Common exceptions in Selenium

You may encounter below types of exceptions and errors when working with Selenium in PHP

1. Element is not clickable at point ....This exception comes when Selenium is not able to click on the element as it is hidden or wrapped in other html tag. To fix this issue, you need to use native JavaScript click method.
2. No Such Element.....This exception comes when element is not found in the web page matching given locator. To prevent this exception, make sure that you have given correct xpath, css selector. Also make sure that element actually exists on the page.
3. The path to the driver executable must be set by the webdriver.chrome.driver system property........This error comes when driver exe file is not found in the system Path or in JVM argument. To fix this issue, you need to make sure that exe file is present in system path.
4. Stale Element Exception - This exception comes when you try to access the element which is loaded afresh in the page. To fix this issue, you need to call findElement method to get the reference to fresh element.
5. IE issues - When trying to launch the IE browser, you may encounter error saying protected mode settings are not same for all security zones. To prevent this issue, you need to make sure that protected mode settings are same for all zones in IE.

# 14. Frameworks in Selenium

## 14.1 Taking a screenshot in selenium

Below example shows how to taking a screenshot using selenium in PHP.

```php
<?php
class MyTest extends
PHPUnit_Framework_TestCase
{
protected $driver;
public function setUp()
{
$capabilities =
array(\WebDriverCapabilityType::BROWSER_NAM
E => 'chrome');
$this->driver =
RemoteWebDriver::create('http://localhost:4
444/wd/hub', $capabilities);
$this->driver->manage()->window()-
>maximize();
}
public function testScreenshot()
{
$this->driver-
>get("http://www.softpost.org/selenium-
test-page");
//Set the path of screenshot file. Here we
have used mt_rand() function to generate
random file name
$screenshotFilePath = mt_rand() .
"abc.png";
$this->driver-
>takeScreenshot($screenshotFilePath);
}
```

```
public function tearDown()
{

//Quit the driver

$this->driver->quit();
}
}
?>
```

## 14.2 Integration with BDD framework like behat

This topic covers how to write the Selenium tests in behat (BDD framework just like cucumber).

Just follow below steps.

1. Create composer.json file and mention all dependencies. Then install all dependencies.
2. Create a features directory and store features in it.
3. Create step definitions.

## **Installing all dependencies**

Create composer.json file with below contents.

```
{
"require-dev": {
"phpunit/phpunit": "*",
"facebook/webdriver": "dev-master",
"behat/behat": "2.4.*@stable"
},
"minimum-stability": "dev",
"config": {
"bin-dir": "bin/"
```

```
}
}
```

Then install the dependencies using composer.

php composer.phar install

## Creating feature file

Then Create features directory and create a feature file in it.

Feature: Title check of pages

Scenario: Check that the title of the home page is "Tutorial"

Given I am on the "http://www.softpost.org" webpage
Then I verify that title contains "Tutorial"

## Creating step definitions

Then create a bootstrap directory inside features directory and store FeatureContext.php file in it. This file contains step definitions.

```
<?php
use Behat\Behat\Context\BehatContext,
Behat\Behat\Exception\PendingException;
use Behat\Gherkin\Node\PyStringNode,
Behat\Gherkin\Node\TableNode;
class FeatureContext extends BehatContext {
protected $driver;
/** @BeforeScenario */
public function before($event)
{
$capabilities =
array(\WebDriverCapabilityType::BROWSER_NAM
```

```
E => 'chrome');
$this->driver =
RemoteWebDriver::create('http://localhost:4
444/wd/hub', $capabilities);
}
/**
* @Given /^I am on the "([^"]*)" webpage$/
*/
public function iAmOnTheWebpage($page)
{
$this->driver->get($page);
}
/**
* @Then /^I verify that title contains
"([^"]*)"$/
*/
public function
iVerifyThatTitleContains($title)
{

// checking that page title contains word
'Tutorial'

PHPUnit_Framework_TestCase::assertContains(
$title, $this->driver->getTitle());
}
/** @AfterScenario */
public function after($event)
{
$this->driver->quit();
}
}
?>
```

To execute the features, you can use below syntax.

bin/behat

www.ingramcontent.com/pod-product-compliance
Lightning Source LLC
Chambersburg PA
CBHW070900070326
40690CB00009B/1925

* 9 7 8 1 5 4 0 6 7 2 9 7 1 *